VIDEO GAMES

STRATEGY GAMES

T0010154

BY ROBERT LEROSE

Apex is distributed by North Star Editions:
sales@northstareditions.com | 888-417-0195

Produced for Apex by Red Line Editorial.

Photographs ©: Shutterstock Images, cover, 1, 4–5, 6, 7, 8, 9, 10–11, 12, 13, 14–15, 18–19, 22–23, 26, 27, 29; Jae C. Hong/AP Images, 16–17; ArcadeImages/Alamy, 20–21; United Archives/Newscom, 24–25

Library of Congress Control Number: 2022920698

ISBN
978-1-63738-578-4 (hardcover)
978-1-63738-632-3 (paperback)
978-1-63738-734-4 (ebook pdf)
978-1-63738-686-6 (hosted ebook)

Printed in the United States of America
Mankato, MN
082023

NOTE TO PARENTS AND EDUCATORS

Apex books are designed to build literacy skills in striving readers. Exciting, high-interest content attracts and holds readers' attention. The text is carefully leveled to allow students to achieve success quickly. Additional features, such as bolded glossary words for difficult terms, help build comprehension.

TABLE OF CONTENTS

CHAPTER 1

RULING THE WORLD

A boy begins a game of *Civilization VI*. He studies the map. He builds his first city near water and other **resources**.

In *Civilization VI*, players try to build an empire and rule the world.

Civilization VI lets gamers play as countries and leaders from history.

The boy fights to protect his city. He also sends Warriors and Scouts to explore new places.

FAST FACT

In *Civilization VI*, players can build many types of objects and characters. Each kind has different skills.

Each object or character is called a unit.

WAYS TO WIN

There are several ways to win *Civilization VI.* Players can fight for a military victory. Or, they can try to spread their religion. Players can also win by leading in science or **culture**.

Soon, the boy controls many cities. He works to make them stronger. He travels to other cities and gains **allies**. Before long, he controls the whole map.

Players win a science victory by being first to send people to live on Mars.

Gamers often play strategy games like *Civilization VI* on computers.

9

CHAPTER 2

GAME HISTORY

Strategy games are about making skilled decisions. Many got their start from board games like chess. Players must plan their moves carefully.

Like strategy video games, chess requires careful thinking and planning to win.

The first strategy video game came out in 1972. It was called *Invasion*. Players moved squares on a TV screen to fight battles. But part of the game still used a board.

Invasion was based on the board game Risk. In Risk, players roll dice to fight and take land.

Eastern Front (1941) is based on fighting that really took place in Russia.

ACTUAL BATTLES

Some strategy games are based on real events. For example, *Eastern Front (1941)* came out in 1981. Players fight in part of World War II (1939–1945).

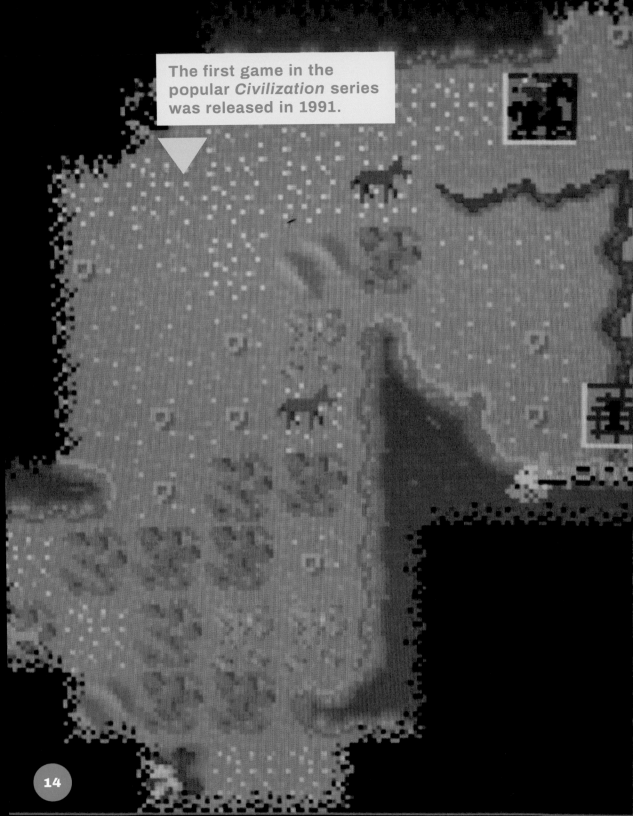

The first game in the popular *Civilization* series was released in 1991.

As computers improved, strategy games did, too. By the 1990s, several games were popular. One was *Dune II*. It was based on a famous sci-fi story.

FAST FACT

Some games let players make **custom** maps and battles.

CHAPTER 3

WAYS TO PLAY

There are several types of strategy games. In some games, players take turns making moves. But in real-time strategy games, all players act at once.

Protoss Probe

Kills: 0

20/20 20

StarCraft is a popular real-time strategy game.

In grand strategy games, each player runs a country. They manage its resources and government. They also interact with other countries. They may trade, fight, or make deals.

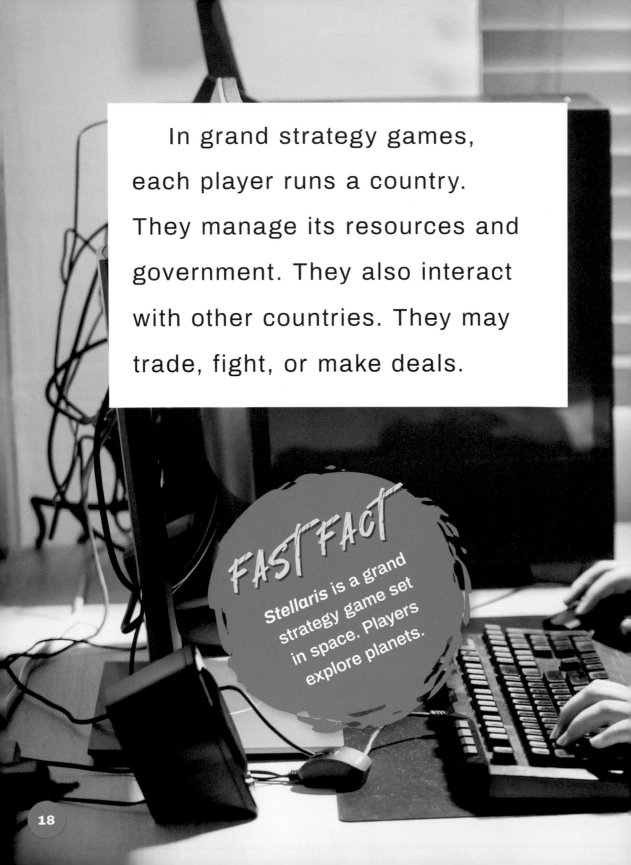

FAST FACT

Stellaris is a grand strategy game set in space. Players explore planets.

People can play grand strategy games against friends. Or they can play alone. A computer controls the other countries.

X-COM: UFO Defense is a turn-based tactics game. Players fight aliens.

Other games focus on **tactics**. In these games, players control an army. They try to win battles.

North Africa
FUNDS▶ $4 141 000

BUILD NEW BASE

BASE INFORMATION

SOLDIERS

EQUIP CRAFT

BUILD FACILITIES

TYPES OF TACTICS

Some tactics games use turns. Others are real-time strategy games. The units **vary**, too. Players may control individual soldiers. Or they may move and fight units in groups.

CHAPTER 4

4X GAMES

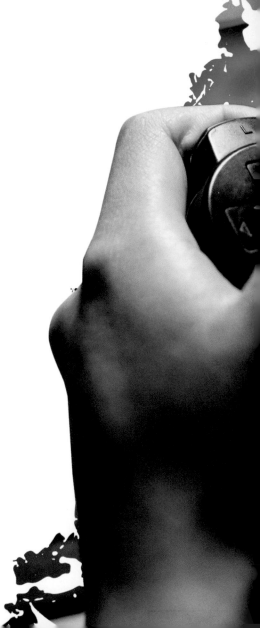

Another popular type of strategy game is 4X. In 4X games, players try to build an empire. They have four main goals.

4X games are often grand strategy and turn based.
But they don't have to be.

First, players explore. They find a place to start their empire. Second, players expand their empire. To do so, they build and fight.

FAST FACT

The first 4X game was *Reach for the Stars*. It came out in 1983.

In 4X games, players often create huge cities and armies.

To expand, players need resources. So, the third goal is to exploit. This means getting resources from the land they control. Fourth, players fight to **exterminate** opponents.

To win *Age of Empires IV*, players must lead their empire through four stages of size and power.

The *Civilization* games are 4X games.

STRANGE WORLD

Endless Legend is a turn-based 4X game. It takes place on a made-up planet. Players try to take over the world. They use armies, science, and **diplomats** to win.

COMPREHENSION QUESTIONS

Write your answers on a separate piece of paper.

1. Write a few sentences describing the main ideas of Chapter 2.

2. Would you rather play a turn-based game or a real-time strategy game? Why?

3. When did the first strategy video game come out?

    A. 1941
    B. 1972
    C. 1981

4. What are the four goals in a 4X game?

    A. explore, earn, eat, exploit
    B. explore, expand, exploit, exit
    C. explore, expand, exploit, exterminate

5. What does **manage** mean in this book?

In grand strategy games, each player runs a country. They manage its resources and government.

    A. be in charge of
    B. be afraid of
    C. be attacked by

6. What does **individual** mean in this book?

Players may control individual soldiers. Or they may move and fight units in groups.

    A. peaceful
    B. single
    C. many at once

Answer key on page 32.

GLOSSARY

allies
People or countries that agree to work together.

culture
A group's way of living, including the art made by its people.

custom
Made or changed to fit a certain goal or plan.

diplomats
Government workers who help make deals with other countries.

exterminate
To get rid of completely.

resources
Important supplies such as food, money, or building materials.

tactics
Plans for fighting and winning battles.

vary
To look or be different.

TO LEARN MORE

BOOKS

Holmes, Kirsty. *Strategy Games*. New York: Crabtree
Publishing Company, 2019.

Rathburn, Betsy. *Computer Gaming*. Minneapolis: Bellwether
Media, 2021.

Tulien, Sean. *Video Games: A Graphic History*. Minneapolis:
Lerner Publishing, 2021.

ONLINE RESOURCES

Visit **www.apexeditions.com** to find links and resources
related to this title.

ABOUT THE AUTHOR

Robert Lerose first learned about video games from two
special players, his niece and nephew. They introduced him
to *Star Fox* and taught him about *Club Penguin*. They can still
take their uncle in any game.

INDEX

ANSWER KEY:
1. Answers will vary; 2. Answers will vary; 3. B; 4. C; 5. A; 6. B